WASP

WASP

a play by

RHIANNON COLLETT

PLAYWRIGHTS CANADA PRESS
TORONTO

First edition: November 2022
Printed and bound in Canada by Rapido Books, Montreal

Cover art by Kira Buro
Author photo by Phimo Photo

Playwrights Canada Press
202-269 Richmond St. W., Toronto, ON M5V 1X1
416.703.0013 | info@playwrightscanada.com | www.playwrightscanada.com

For professional or amateur production rights, please contact:
Colin Rivers at Marquis Entertainment
402–10 Adelaide St. East, Toronto, ON M5C 1J3
416-960-9123 x 223 | info@mqlit.ca

LIBRARY AND ARCHIVES CANADA CATALOGUING IN PUBLICATION
Title: Wasp / a play by Rhiannon Collett.
Names: Collett, Rhiannon, author.
Identifiers: Canadiana (print) 20220446113 | Canadiana (ebook) 2022044613X
| ISBN 9780369102997 (softcover) | ISBN 9780369103017 (EPUB)
| ISBN 9780369103000 (PDF)
Classification: LCC PS8605.04555 W37 2022 | DDC C812/.6—dc23

Playwrights Canada Press operates on land which is the ancestral home of the Anishinaabe Nations (Ojibwe / Chippewa, Odawa, Potawatomi, Algonquin, Saulteaux, Nipissing, and Mississauga), the Wendat, and the members of the Haudenosaunee Confederacy (Mohawk, Oneida, Onondaga, Cayuga, Seneca, and Tuscarora), as well as Metis and Inuit peoples. It always was and always will be Indigenous land.

We acknowledge the support of the Canada Council for the Arts, the Ontario Arts Council (OAC), Ontario Creates, and the Government of Canada for our publishing activities.

Canada Council for the Arts | Conseil des arts du Canada

ONTARIO ARTS COUNCIL
CONSEIL DES ARTS DE L'ONTARIO
an Ontario government agency
un organisme du gouvernement de l'Ontario

Canada

ONTARIO CREATES | ONTARIO CRÉATIF

For Jess

Wasp was commissioned and developed with the support of Nightswimming. Further support was provided by the Toronto Arts Council, the Canada Council for the Arts, the Rhubarb Festival (Buddies in Bad Times Theatre), the Stratford Festival Laboratory, lemonTree creations, and safeword. A twenty-five-minute excerpt of the piece was presented at the 2019 Rhubarb Festival (Buddies in Bad Times, Toronto), featuring Heath V. Salazar as Wasp, Gabe Maharjan as Janey, Robin Luckwaldt as Caroline, and Cole Alvis as Isaac, directed/written/produced by Rhiannon Collett, sound design by James Knott, and dramaturgy by Brian Quirt.

The play was developed as an audio drama in 2022, co-produced by safeword and Harlot X, in affiliation with Nightswimming, featuring Robin Luckwaldt as Wasp, Cole Alvis as Janey, Brefny Caribou as Rachel, Jillian Harris as Caroline, and Heath V. Salazar as Isaac. It was co-directed by Rhiannon Collett and Gabe Maharjan, produced by Brandon Crone and Rhiannon Collett, with production dramaturgy by Gabe Maharjan and Brian Quirt, sound design and audio production by Ren Bangert, and stage management by Katherine Belyea.

GLOSSARY

The Church of the Angel Redeemers: A.k.a., the Cult. A fundamentalist group that hopes to expand and homogenize the town's population through Angelic intervention.

The Angels: A swarm of yellowjackets that impregnate uterus-havers with rapid twelve-hour pregnancies.

Divine Birthday: The day that a virgin and a man join together to offer their bodies to the Angels through a special ritual at the Altar.

The Altar: The cult building where all rituals take place.

Holy Mother: A virgin in the cult who chooses (or is told) to give her reproductive power to the Angels.

Seraphim: Men in the cult who choose (or are told) to give their reproductive power to the angels.

Coca-Cola: A last-ditch attempt at abortion access.

CHARACTERS

Wasp (they/them): Non-binary person, mid-twenties. Janey's boyfriend, Isaac's ex-girlfriend.

Janey (she/her): Transgender woman, early in transition. Mid-twenties. Wasp's girlfriend.

Rachel (she/her): Cisgender woman. Early twenties. Lesbian. Caroline's sister. Younger daughter of the Prophet.

Caroline (she/her): Cisgender woman. Mid-twenties. Isaac's girlfriend, Rachel's sister. Older daughter of the Prophet.

Isaac (he/him): Cisgender man. Mid-to-late twenties. Caroline's boyfriend, Wasp's ex-boyfriend.

The Prophet (he/him): Cisgender man, late fifties. The leader of the Church of the Angel Redeemers. Rachel and Caroline's father. Never seen, only heard.

THE SETTING

A small town in Northern BC. Mountainous. Forested. Isolated but still within driving distance of a major city.

A NOTE ABOUT PRONOUNS

As Janey and Wasp are living their lives semi-stealth (read: not out as trans), the other characters often misgender and/or deadname them. In an effort to acknowledge the impact that deadnaming can have on trans people, I have redacted Janey's deadname, with the characters referring to her as "J—."

A NOTE ABOUT CASTING & PRODUCTION

Wasp is a love letter to my trans community. This means trans people need to be part of every step of production. Trans producers, trans directors, trans actors. We're here. We're talented. Hire us.

If you, like me, have felt lost in a theatrical ecosystem that prioritizes respectability over artistic risk, listen: our stories are alive in ways they will never understand. Fuck professionalism, fuck palatability, fuck toning it down.

Fuck the cult of heteronormativity and all the ways it plays out in our lives.

[ACT I, SCENE I]

An abandoned church on the side of a highway, somewhere in Northern BC. *The sanctuary is littered with toppled pews and torn hymn books. Light filters in through cracked stained glass. Pieces of a giant organ emerge from the gloom like reeds. The toll of a church bell—it's 10 a.m.* ISAAC *builds a pyramid of empty Coke bottles. It's clear he's been drinking.*

There's only one unopened bottle of Coke left. He goes to open it, but a knock on the door catches him off guard.

ISAAC: Coming, coming!

CAROLINE: *(from outside)* Since when does this door have a lock on it?

ISAAC *scrambles to put the Coke bottles away—he knocks over his drink in the process.* CAROLINE *knocks louder.*

ISAAC: I said I'm coming!

ISAAC *opens the door.* CAROLINE *stands in the doorway. She's dressed plainly but oozes charisma.*

CAROLINE: Hi, Daddy. Did you miss me?

ISAAC: I always miss you.

CAROLINE: Really. I thought we were meeting at your house.

ISAAC: Yeah, babe, at 9:30.

CAROLINE: It's 10. The bell just rang.
Where's your phone? I called you like fifty times.

ISAAC: Shit. It's dead. I lost track of time. I was working on renovations.

It's clear he hasn't been renovating anything.

CAROLINE: Right. Renovations.

She kisses him and then pulls away.

Back on the breakfast rum and Coke I see.

ISAAC: Don't kiss me like that.

CAROLINE: Like what?

ISAAC: Like a sniffer dog. It's a greeting, not a taste test.

CAROLINE: It's rotting your teeth straight out of your head. Father put it in here for safekeeping, not as your personal vending machine.

ISAAC: They're not gonna miss a few bottles.

CAROLINE: It's disturbing. An ungodly beverage.

ISAAC: But the rum's okay?

CAROLINE: No. It's not. None of it is okay. No rum, no Coke, no ditching me, no nothing!

ISAAC: Okay, *Jesus*.

Beat.

Christ is our Lord and Saviour. Amen.

CAROLINE: *(laughing despite herself)* Amen. Nice catch. *(getting closer to him)* You know I worry about you.

ISAAC: I know. But I'm on the path. Cross my heart, baby.

He kisses her again. She relaxes a bit.

CAROLINE: I picked up your suit from the dry cleaner. It's in the car.

Beat.

Are you sure there isn't anyone you want to invite?

ISAAC: Did you talk to your dad?

CAROLINE: Not my dad, Isaac. The Prophet.

ISAAC: Did you talk to *the Prophet*?

CAROLINE: I did. He was overjoyed that you're taking such initiative already.

ISAAC: You're mad.

CAROLINE: I'm not mad. I just—I thought we'd get some time to ourselves. Just our little family.

ISAAC: You and me come first, Caro. But this looks really good—two in one night? Think about it. It's powerful.

Beat.

So I have his permission?

CAROLINE: He added it to your covenant. She's scheduled for midnight. But I'm first.

ISAAC: Of course.

CAROLINE: I don't know why you both think she should get special treatment.

ISAAC: She's a hard sell. I've never met anyone more stubborn.

CAROLINE: I'm stubborn. You don't coddle me.

ISAAC: Caroline . . .

CAROLINE: *(ignoring him)* What kind of name is Wasp, anyway?

ISAAC: Babe. Don't be like this. She doesn't mean anything to me. I just . . . I think I could bag her. I want your dad—*the Prophet*—to know I'm committed. You too.

CAROLINE: It's a lot, Isaac. No one's ever done two in one night before.

ISAAC: You know I have the stamina.

CAROLINE: Okay.

She sets two pills down on the table. They're black-and-yellow striped. She kisses one and hands it to him.

This one's mine.

ISAAC: Bottoms up.

He finishes the rest of his drink. CAROLINE *watches him. She has doubts.*

CAROLINE: Maybe I can talk to J—? Tag team?

ISAAC: Great idea.

You know the only reason I'm taking "initiative" is because I had the best tutor in town.

She doesn't reply. He continues:

She's the most beautiful, most devout, most pure tutor in all the land. A glowing receptacle for God's light and love. And she's going to be an amazing mom.

CAROLINE: Oh yeah?

ISAAC: Uh huh. She was born for this.

ISAAC kisses her neck. CAROLINE turns to him.

CAROLINE: I'm so excited, baby. I went to the store today and I got these little socks. Blue.

ISAAC: You think it's gonna be a boy?

CAROLINE: I think he's gonna be perfect perfect.

He puts his hand on her stomach.

ISAAC: Perfect perfect.

He continues kissing her neck—she leans into him. It's clear they have a way of doing things. He grabs her hair, starts to push her head down for a blow job.

CAROLINE: Isaac, not now.

ISAAC: What? I thought you said oral doesn't count.

CAROLINE: Yeah, but not today. God's here.

ISAAC: Here?

He unzips his fly. She can feel him.

CAROLINE: Here.

She points at the stained glass.

ISAAC: I mean, I could go down on you.

Shockingly, he's still trying to get her to have sex. He lifts up the hem of her skirt. She stops him.

CAROLINE: Tomorrow. Today is for the Angels only.

ISAAC: You'll be pregnant tomorrow. Now's our last chance.

CAROLINE: Last chance before what? Before my vagina looks like the deli section at Phil's?

ISAAC: That was a joke, Caroline—

CAROLINE: Lacey's still hot and she's had like three Divine Birthdays. She even gave me a stretch-mark cream. You're still going to find me sexy, right? Even after?

Beat. ISAAC *doesn't know what to say.*

Compliment me!

ISAAC: You have a perfect ass. And soul.

CAROLINE: And you'll still find me sexy?

ISAAC: Of course. You're sexy forever, Mama.

CAROLINE: I keep thinking about the moment. The doors'll open and you'll walk in, pulsing with heavenly light.

ISAAC: Pulsing, huh?

CAROLINE: You'll be filled with their power. They'll just pour out of you.

ISAAC: God, I love your fantasies.

CAROLINE: The hum. The thrust of your hips as we conceive. The applause.

ISAAC: Applause?

CAROLINE: The community applauds when you climax. It's in the handbook.

ISAAC: Must have not gotten to that part yet.

CAROLINE sighs.

CAROLINE: What am I ever going to do with you, Isaac?

ISAAC: I have some ideas.

[ACT I, SCENE 2]

JANEY is at Phil's, the grocery store-cum-garden-centre-cum-gas-station-cum-pharmacy run by the Church of the Angel Redeemers. She waits for a while. On the counter there's a small rotating fan and a stack of religious pamphlets. Jehovah's Witnesses–style, if they weren't being covert. On the front a faggot burns in Hell. On the back, a number to call. JANEY flips through one of them. Nothing she hasn't seen before. Finally, annoyed, she leans over the counter.

JANEY: Ding ding ding. Anybody home? Helloooooo?

We hear the sound of raised voices—suddenly RACHEL appears, flustered, from the back room. She speaks stiffly to JANEY as if she's afraid of being overheard.

RACHEL: Oh, hi, J—.

JANEY: Salutations.

RACHEL: Have you been waiting long?

JANEY: I've waited longer.

JANEY waves a pamphlet jokingly.

All caught up on the new lit. Some veeeeery interesting stuff you have here. You don't mind if I take a few, do you?

RACHEL: Are you going to read them?

JANEY: Better than that: I'm going to give them to every faggot I know. Here you go.

> *She makes a movement like she's going to hand one to* RACHEL. RACHEL *doesn't laugh.*

RACHEL: *(under her breath)* If you're going to throw them in the dumpster . . . can you choose another one? Like . . . not the one behind the building?

JANEY: I mean I guess I could always burn them.

RACHEL: *(tightly)* Sure. That would be great.

(louder) Is there something I can help you with, sir?

> *She emphasizes the "sir."* JANEY *is irritated but understands it's not time to play around.*

JANEY: I'm here for my meds, ma'am.

RACHEL: I don't have any prescriptions on file for you.

JANEY: I'm here for Wasp's medication. I have their ID if you want.

> RACHEL *talks as if she's reading a script, but like she might cry at any moment.*

RACHEL: I'm afraid we can't help you with that. They've been deprioritized.

JANEY: Deprioritized? It's birth control.

RACHEL: You know how bad the roads have been. Recently. With the flooding, the forest fires, the—

JANEY: I get it. Bad driving. So?

RACHEL: So there's been a back order on certain medications.

JANEY: "Certain medications."

RACHEL: They had to make some decisions, what with the limited shipments. Some things didn't make the cut. May I offer you a condom?

> *RACHEL pulls a basket of condoms out from behind the desk. They each have a price tag: twenty-five dollars.*

JANEY: What am I supposed to do, choke on it?

RACHEL: Janey. Not today.

JANEY: Okay. Shipping delays. Sure.

So. When's it coming back in?

RACHEL: Not for a while.

JANEY: How long is a while?

RACHEL: Until they get things under control.

> *JANEY stares at the cross hanging on the wall behind the pharmacy.*

JANEY: Holy fucking shit.

RACHEL: Please don't swear. They'll kick you out again.

JANEY: Wow. Wow.

> *JANEY turns to leave but then hesitates. She's desperate.*

I'm almost out. Tomorrow. Do you have any like . . . left over, from the last time you ordered?

RACHEL: Have you tried turning to God for your condemned urges?

JANEY: What, did they give you a script?

RACHEL: Have a nice day, sir.

JANEY: *(under her breath)* When's your next break?

RACHEL: Now.

JANEY: Have a nice day, ma'am.

> *RACHEL doesn't answer. JANEY walks out of Phil's and crosses the street, next to the crematorium. She stands in the alley and lights a cigarette. After a few moments, RACHEL comes out the front door and crosses to meet her. JANEY hands her a cigarette.*

(waving the pamphlets) Should we start a dumpster fire, or?

RACHEL: You can't come back again. At least not while I'm working. It's not safe. They know.

JANEY: Know what?

RACHEL: Too much.

JANEY: Not everyone in this town wants to drink their fucking Kool-Aid.

RACHEL: They know that. But wouldn't you want the Kool-Aid just a little bit more if you were pregnant and alone?

JANEY: They still have condoms.

RACHEL: Don't buy the condoms. Last shift I stapled every package.

Beat.

JANEY: Fuck. You gotta get out of there.

RACHEL: Great advice. Hadn't thought of that.

Beat.

You're not gonna die without it, right? The birth control.

JANEY: Sure.

RACHEL: So you'll be all right?

JANEY: I mean. I'll be hairier. And my tits will disappear. And my testosterone will spike. And I'll be wildly suicidal. But yeah. I'll be fine.

RACHEL: Just another hairy, flat-chested girl bent on self-destruction. What do you think, should we get T-shirts?

JANEY: *(suddenly angry)* It's not a fucking joke, Rachel. It's my life.

Beat.

RACHEL: You're right, it's not a joke. I'm sorry.
You're just the first outsider I've spoken to in weeks.
I feel like I'm losing it.

JANEY: Join the club.

RACHEL: It's awful without you. Caroline's fully absorbed everything our dad says. Even when he's not there, she's like, "Prophet this, Prophet that." It's like living with two crazy people.

JANEY: So leave!

RACHEL: I'm trying! I know your life sucks, but so does mine. I was in a disciplinary meeting when you came in. They wanted me to test the script on you.

JANEY: You're a great actor.

RACHEL: Oh fuck off.

JANEY: So which sin was it? Lying, forgeing . . . tardiness?

RACHEL: Sodomy.

JANEY raises her eyebrows.

JANEY: *Really.*

RACHEL: Yeah. Her name was Sarah. Which I thought was funny, you know, like, Sarah and Abraham. An unfertile woman. A miracle conception.

JANEY: Was she also like ninety-nine years old and living in a tent?

RACHEL: She was just passing through. Her hair smelled like strawberries.

Beat.

Did you know you can fit your whole hand inside a vagina?

JANEY: You fisted her?

RACHEL: Yeah. Knuckles and all. I was scared I'd hurt her, but the look on her face. Those big brown eyes looking up at me. Damn.

Beat.

We did it in my dad's office. Caroline saw us through the stained-glass window.

JANEY: She didn't.

RACHEL: She did. Ran right to Daddy.

Beat.

Predictable, but still disappointing.

JANEY: I mean, sodomy in the Prophet's office seems like a great reason to get kicked out of the church. That's way worse than one little cross-dressing incident.

RACHEL *inhales shakily—she's trying not to cry.*

RACHEL: It didn't work. We should have done it in the sanctuary. Or maybe I should have fucked her with the cross. Pissed in the baptismal font—whatever.

Beat.

I can't get out.

They're low on . . . I don't know, uteruses? Babies? Servile women?

Beat.

They were telling me about my new accommodations when you walked in. My chaperones. My curfew. I think they're gonna fast-track me to the Divine Birthday. And, yeah, there's no more birth control. I was taking it too. Sorry.

RACHEL digs around in her bag, pulls out a half-used package of birth control.

Take it. You need it more than me.

JANEY: *(touched)* Rachel.

RACHEL: It doesn't work on Angels anyway. No normal pregnancy for me.

Beat.

You look good, Janey. Sorry for deadnaming you.

JANEY: It's okay.

RACHEL: Have you heard from Caroline?

JANEY: Not for a long time. She excels at the whole shunning thing.

RACHEL: It's her turn tonight. Isaac's getting converted. He's gonna take her.

JANEY: They're making Isaac a Seraphim?

RACHEL: I filled his prescription this morning. Locked and loaded.

JANEY: Gross.

RACHEL: Like I said, they're desperate.

Beat.

I gotta go back to work. I'm glad you got out, even if I'm lonely.

JANEY: I'm still here. Don't worry.

RACHEL stubs out her cigarette, kisses JANEY on the cheek, and crosses the street. JANEY looks at the birth control for a long moment. She's overcome by the urge to DO SOMETHING—throw a brick, storm in there and kidnap RACHEL, break something. The feeling moves through her body—and settles in her chest. She heads towards her bike, Big Sexy, that she's parked down the street.

Suddenly we hear horrible Christian music and the sound of a car approaching. CAROLINE is driving and she pulls over next to JANEY.

(as she sees her approaching) No fucking way.

CAROLINE: J—, J—! Wait up!

JANEY: *(picking up speed)* No. No no no no no.

At this point JANEY is speed walking and CAROLINE is rolling along beside her in the car. Her driving is stressful: if there was a mailbox, she'd hit it.

CAROLINE: Hi! How've you been?

JANEY doesn't reply.

Not even a hello?

JANEY: I thought you were ignoring me.

CAROLINE: Clearly you're ignoring *me*.

JANEY keeps walking.

J—. J—! Can you stop just for a second? I wanted to show you something.

JANEY keeps walking until she reaches Big Sexy. She starts to unhook her helmet. CAROLINE stops the car and jumps out. She has something clutched in her hand. She thrusts it towards JANEY.

Look at this!

She hands JANEY a very old, very stinky egg.

(with bated breath) We're in, J—. He took his vow. Signed the covenant and everything. You said it couldn't be done. But here we are!

JANEY: *(handing the egg back)* Congratulations on your rotten egg.

CAROLINE: He's ready, you know. All my work paid off. Isaac took this egg everywhere he went for three weeks! Three whole weeks! Not a crack.

JANEY: Ah yes, the old "baby as egg" method. Tried and true parenting.

CAROLINE: He sat on like five of them the first week, but then he got the hang of it. This egg is thriving. And babies make noise, so it's a lot harder to forget where you put them.

JANEY: Nice to hear about your upcoming motherhood, but I have somewhere to be.

CAROLINE: Where?

JANEY: Anywhere but here. Bye!

JANEY swings her leg up over Big Sexy. She starts the bike and pulls away. CAROLINE hurls the egg at her. It cracks and runs down Janey's back. She turns the bike off.

CAROLINE: Are you not happy for me?

JANEY: Did you just *egg* me with your metaphorical child?

CAROLINE: I need to talk to you. Stop running away.

JANEY: I'm not running away! I'm going home. You do realize that six months have passed since you so much as looked at me, right?

CAROLINE: I had to be on my best behaviour while I prepared for my Divine Birthday. My candidacy was at risk. No sinners. I thought you'd understand.

JANEY: Oh fuck you!

CAROLINE: Since when do you curse?

JANEY: Since when do you care? Brown-noser.

CAROLINE: Heretic.

JANEY: Loser.

Beat. CAROLINE *collects herself.*

CAROLINE: I wanted to extend an invite to you, for tonight.

I'm allowed to invite two outsiders, and I thought that maybe you and Wasp could come and see the miracle. Maybe it'll change your mind.

JANEY: No thanks.

CAROLINE: Come on. It'll be just like old times.

JANEY: Watching you and Isaac fuck on a rock is not "just like old times."

CAROLINE: *(ignoring her)* Nobody sits in your pew. I think they're waiting for you to come back. You could take the interview again. Prove that you're pure of heart.

JANEY: I am pure of heart. That's the problem.

CAROLINE: You need to repent.

JANEY: What I actually need is to get the egg off my jacket.

CAROLINE: Sorry. I got carried away. Here.

> CAROLINE *grabs a cloth out of the trunk and hands it to* JANEY. JANEY *wipes the egg off her coat and goes to throw it back in the trunk.*

Watch the dress!

JANEY: The dress?

> JANEY *looks in the trunk—inside there's a dry cleaning bag, and through the plastic she can see the ritual dress. Her breath catches in her throat. She's always fantasized about the dress.*

CAROLINE: Do you wanna see?

> *She pulls it out of the bag, holds it up to* JANEY*'s chest.* JANEY *is mesmerized.*

It's gorgeous, isn't it?

JANEY: It's a little more blood-stained than I remember.

CAROLINE: It's old. Do you remember how good Lacey looked in it before she went to the Altar?

JANEY: Yeah. I thought she was like a princess or something.

CAROLINE: She had an easy labour. She said the pregnancy's so fast your body just snaps back into place when you're done. I hope it's like that for me.

Beat. JANEY *keeps staring at the dress.*

I was thinking, you should come over. I need someone to curl my hair.

JANEY: I don't know how.

CAROLINE: I'll teach you.

JANEY: Why don't you ask Rachel?

CAROLINE: She's on the clock.

JANEY: Desperate times call for desperate measures.

CAROLINE: No. Not desperate measures. Best friend measures. Just two friends, engaging in the ancient art form of—

JANEY: Preparing for ritual sacrifice?

CAROLINE: Preparing for the future.

JANEY: *(almost tempted)* Caroline . . .

CAROLINE: . . . Please? Please come. It'd mean the world.

JANEY *holds the dress to her chest. She slips her arms through the sleeves. She twirls in it.* CAROLINE *notices and tries to grab it back. A subtle keep-away game ensues.*

You have those slacks I bought you, right? And the blue button up?

JANEY: I threw them out. Blue isn't really my colour.

CAROLINE: What are you doing?

CAROLINE *grabs at the dress.* JANEY *scoots away.*

JANEY: What do you think? Will Wasp like it? They mostly eat eggs for breakfast, but it's part of a balanced diet, and I think they'd make a good dad.

CAROLINE: That's enough. Take that off. Someone's going to see.

JANEY: Maybe we can go together. Give each other the ritual bath. Hold hands?

JANEY touches CAROLINE's hand. CAROLINE pulls away.

CAROLINE: This isn't some game, J—. Take it off.

JANEY's deadname jolts her back down to earth. She realizes how dangerous she's being right now. She tries to take the dress off— the zipper is stuck. She starts to panic, feeling claustrophobic.

JANEY: The zipper's stuck.

CAROLINE: Stay still!

CAROLINE unzips her.

You need a haircut. Slick it back tonight and you'll look just like your old self.

Beat. CAROLINE looks at the dress.

What were you thinking?

JANEY: I don't know.

JANEY starts her bike. CAROLINE steps back. The dress blows in the breeze; she clutches it to avoid the dirt JANEY kicks up. The roar of the motorcycle crescendos. It cuts to silence.

[ACT I, SCENE 3]

WASP and JANEY are in the kitchen of their home. WASP unloads a tote bag and dumps an armload of zucchini onto the table.

WASP: Zucchini.

JANEY: Nooooooo! I told you. I'm on strike. No more. No more loaf, no more ratatouille, no more stir-fry . . .

WASP: I hear they're good in muffins.

JANEY: Please . . . have mercy . . .

WASP: It's all we've got. The garden's overgrown again. I spent six hours weeding yesterday, and you can't tell. I don't think the carrots are gonna make it.

JANEY: Who knew they were such a little bitch of a vegetable.

WASP: Yeah. I miss weeding parties.

JANEY: I miss parties.

WASP: Call Rachel. Tell her it's a zucchini emergency.

JANEY: She's locked down. New curfew. Parties of three are now parties of two.

WASP: That's really gonna fuck up spin the bottle.

JANEY: Very funny.

WASP hands JANEY a knife and a cutting board. They kiss her.

WASP: Start chopping.

JANEY's phone rings. It's CAROLINE. She shows WASP.

JANEY: The audacity. What is this, Hotline Caroline?

WASP: We could get high and watch her fuck Isaac at the Altar. A little live-action porno.

JANEY: I would absolutely never recover. Plus, she wanted me to wear loafers. LOAFERS. That girl is unhinged.

WASP: I mean she did let you try on the dress.

JANEY: I wouldn't call it "letting me." More like I molested it while she watched in horror.

WASP: Still. I bet you looked cute.

JANEY: Not in the eyes of God.

WASP: Nonsense. God loves us.

JANEY's phone buzzes. It's another text from CAROLINE.

JANEY: Apparently I'm supposed to come over for seven.

Beat.

They're running us out.

WASP: They're trying to make us breeders. Clearly they don't know how lesbians have sex. Should we tell them P in V is cancelled?

JANEY: Well then they're running me out.

WASP: There's no way they'd know what you were using birth control for.

JANEY: Right. No difference. Same old man body.

WASP: That's not what I meant. I just don't think they're targeting you.

WASP takes the zucchini from JANEY. JANEY is silent.

Janey . . . you look good. Really good. It's making a difference.

JANEY rolls her eyes.

JANEY: What is it, my sallow, defeated skin? Or the dark circles under my eyes?

WASP: That's from stress, not from testosterone. Your skin looks bright.

JANEY: Liar.

WASP: You have that estrogen glow. Sexy. And your face looks softer. Like you just woke up. Fresh. Cherubic.

JANEY: *(warming up a little)* A transsexual cherub. Hot.

WASP: Yeah. And . . .

They hug her, then run a hand over her chest.

Are your nipples . . . pointier than usual?

JANEY: Pointier?

WASP: More . . . tender, maybe?

JANEY: They are.

Beat.

You noticed? For real?

WASP: I've been watching them grow for weeks. I'm like a titty farmer. Patient, weathered, horny . . .

JANEY: I was going to wait to say something because I didn't think you'd be able to tell, but LOOK.

WASP looks down her shirt. JANEY presses WASP's hand to her chest.

Do you feel that? The bump?

WASP: Yeah. I do. I do!

JANEY: It's breast buds, bitch!

An alarm goes off on JANEY's phone (it's bitch mint o'clock). She remembers again that she's almost out of hormones. She doesn't move.

WASP: What, you're not going to take them?

JANEY: What's the point? I have like a week left. And then it's done.

WASP: The point is it's not done yet.

Beat.

Come on. We'll figure something out.

WASP rustles around in JANEY's bag and pulls out the birth control.

Shall we?

JANEY: Okay.

They both bow their heads.

Dear God, bless this mess.
Let my tits grow big and plentiful through your grace and medication.
May all the testosterone be eradicated from my sexy and furry body.
Protect us from transphobes, cult leaders, and heterosexuals.
In the name of the Mother, the Daughter, and the Holy Cootchie, amen.

WASP: Amen.

A long beat. CAROLINE calls again. WASP picks up the phone and declines the call.

You should block her number.

JANEY: *(miserably)* I know.

WASP: Your hair's growing back in.

JANEY: I don't think it is.

WASP: It is. It'll be down to your ass by the summer.
And then I'll walk you on it like a leash.

They're flirting but JANEY's worried again.

JANEY: Not if it falls out again.
(softly) What am I gonna do, Wasp?

WASP: Do you think Rachel could pull some more strings?

JANEY: They're after her too.

Beat.

I thought it would be different. I knew they'd shun me, but I thought that meant they'd forget, let me fly under the radar. Stupid.

WASP: There's got to be another option.

JANEY: Yeah. I stay here, and I detransition. My body hardens. The hair comes back on my fingers and toes. My beard thickens. My body eats me from the outside in. And then, when my backwards transformation is complete and I have absolutely nothing, they come for me.

WASP: No one's coming for you. They banned birth control because they're a cult, not because they're hunting you down.

JANEY: The Prophet always said that every man becomes a Seraphim when he's ready. Ready. Is that when you give up? Are you just, like, sure I'll become a woman-hating misogynistic piece of shit. Sign me up.

WASP: You're not a man, Janey.

JANEY: Thanks for the fucking news flash!

JANEY gets up and starts to pace the room. She feels trapped in her body—she's on the edge of having a full-blown panic attack.

JANEY: I can't do this. I can't go backwards—I'll kill myself.

WASP: So it's time. We have to leave.

JANEY: No. Fuck that.

WASP: Everyone else already left.

JANEY: Yeah but that wasn't going to be us. This is our home.

WASP: Yeah. It is. And it's killing you.

Listen—I love our home. I love that it's where we grew up. I love the mountains, and the ice-blue river, and the wildflower seeds that you scatter everywhere when you think no one's looking.

JANEY: Public disobedience is hot.

WASP: You practically landscaped the entire highway!

JANEY: Yeah. Highway 97 is now a gay icon.

WASP: I love our bed. Our yellow kitchen. Our matching slippers. But this is insane. You can't even get the actual medication you need. Birth control is a half-assed substitute.

Beat.

I keep thinking you're going to get a blood clot and drop dead.

JANEY: Fingers crossed.

WASP: Don't say that! No dying. Promise.

Beat.

JANEY: I can't.

WASP: So it's time. You can scatter flowers somewhere else.

Beat.

We have a week before your meds run out. We won't tell anyone we're leaving.

JANEY: Not even your gran?

WASP: No. She went back to them. I can't blame her, she's so lonely.

JANEY: I guess this is when being excommunicated from your family comes in handy.

Beat.

Rachel.

WASP: We'll come back for her.

JANEY: We have to.

WASP: We will.

A long pause as they consider RACHEL*'s fate. There's nothing they can do.*

JANEY: Okay. I have next weekend off—we could leave after I finish at the garage, that way no one will notice until at least Monday.

WASP: Yeah, and I'll start talking about feeling sick next shift. That way the diner won't suspect when I call in on Saturday.

JANEY: Big Sexy'll take us as far as we need to go. We're gonna have to pack light though.

WASP: Vroom vroom. We hit the highway and then—we're just a nice straight couple, enjoying a weekend away.

JANEY: No transgender fugitives here, baby. I love to vacation with my wife.

WASP: Should we bring the tent? In case we can't find a motel—

Outside there's a sudden loud crash. We hear the slam of a car door, and then some swearing.

ISAAC: Fuck! Chipped my damn paint job.

JANEY looks out the window. ISAAC is downstairs, standing next to her bike, which looks absolutely mangled.

JANEY: What the FUCK, ISAAC?

ISAAC: I didn't see it! Why'd you park it so far from the house?

JANEY: It's a driveway, you absolute fuck! Put your goddamn glasses on!

JANEY turns back to WASP.

Both of them in one day. I told you. Running us out.

Another crash from outside.

I'm going to kill him. Tell me I shouldn't kill him right now.

(out the window) Get the FUCK OUT OF MY DRIVEWAY!

ISAAC: Wasp—are you there? I need to talk to you.

JANEY: *(out the window)* They're not home. LEAVE.

WASP: Hold on.

JANEY: You're not actually going down there.

WASP: He has four-wheel drive. Tinted windows. No one'll notice us.

JANEY: A stolen car is pretty noticeable.

WASP: So are two faggots on a motorbike!

JANEY: I thought we were straight!

WASP: I'll—I'll get him to give it to me.

JANEY: No. We'll find something else.

WASP: Where? No one is going to lend us anything. We're already too suspicious.

JANEY: We'll rent one.

WASP: With what money?

JANEY: Not him.

WASP: He won't even know we're stealing it. It'll be like taking candy from a baby.

JANEY: A fucking ugly baby.

ISAAC: HELLOOOOO?

WASP: Trust me. I know him. I can do it.

JANEY: *(out the window)* SHUT THE FUCK UP! They're coming!

(to WASP) Be careful.

WASP: Always am.

[ACT I, SCENE 4]

WASP goes downstairs. ISAAC stands next to the mangled motorbike.

ISAAC: I know it looks bad, but it's totally not. Just a dent or two. Easy fix. Hell, bring it to me at the garage on Monday, and I'll fix it myself.

WASP: Tell me what you want before J— comes down and attempts murder.

ISAAC: I have a surprise for you.

ISAAC throws them the keys and gets in the passenger side of his car. WASP hesitates. ISAAC leans out the window.

You're gonna love it. Take the highway. I'll tell you when to turn.

WASP: Fine. But if I'm not back in an hour, J— has my full permission to rip you a new asshole.

ISAAC: He's more than welcome to try.

WASP waves to JANEY through the window—keys in hand. They get in the car and pull out of the driveway. WASP turns the radio on, but immediately a Christian jingle starts playing. We hear the PROPHET's voice through the crackle of the radio.

PROPHET: Do you feel alone? Like other people just don't "get it"? Are you depressed? Missing meaning in your life? We're seeking passionate, playful individuals interested in expanding their spiritual horizons on our gorgeous forty-two-acre farm right off Highway 97—room and board included!—call 1-800—

WASP groans and turns it off.

ISAAC: *(half joking)* What, you don't want to expand your spiritual horizons?

WASP: Not with them.

ISAAC: Caroline keeps trying to sign me up for these Emotional Intelligence Classes. Apparently I need to "process." She says it'll make me a better boyfriend.

WASP: I've said it before, Isaac: you need therapy, not brainwashing.

ISAAC: It's not brainwashing if everyone goes. And you get a professional report card at the end.

WASP: Let me guess, straight As for Caroline?

ISAAC: No letter grades. But she did get the Outstanding Empath Award and a gold star for Maturity.

WASP raises their eyebrows.

We were going through a hard time. Anyway. The Prophet said he thinks I'd succeed.

WASP: Since when have you started calling him the Prophet and not Caroline's creepy dad.

ISAAC: *(shrugs)* It's his title. Anyway, I told Caroline that I was too fucked up for therapy or whatever and she said, "You're not fucked up, you just need God."

WASP: Easy for her to say. God's her best friend.

ISAAC: Yeah. She sure is a firecracker.

WASP: Dangerous?

ISAAC: Bright, pretty, and a little bit explosive. Guess I have a type. It's nice to see you.

> *He puts his hand on their knee. They don't resist—but they do sigh internally: it seems seduction is the way to* ISAAC*'s car.*

WASP: It's nice to see you too.

ISAAC: *(taken aback)* Really?

WASP: You know I think about you. How've you been?

ISAAC: Uh. Good. A bit stressed out, but good. How about you?

WASP: . . . Does it smell like rotten eggs in here?

ISAAC: Nope.

WASP: Should I turn here?

ISAAC: Next one.

> *They sit in silence.* ISAAC*'s hand is still on* WASP*'s leg. They can feel it in their entire body.*

I didn't think . . . you would be like this.

WASP: Like what?

ISAAC: Nice.

WASP laughs.

WASP: Am I being nice?

ISAAC: This is it.

WASP stops the car. They've arrived outside the abandoned church.

WASP: The abandoned church on the side of the highway?

ISAAC: No. *My* abandoned church on the side of the highway.

Beat.

It's even better inside, come on. Keys.

He opens his hand for the keys. WASP hesitates before handing them over. ISAAC grabs their hand and leads them inside, into the sanctuary. It's in disarray and completely filthy. There's a dirty mattress on the floor. He gives them a tour. There's a kitchen, a bathroom, a children's play area. The electricity works, but barely. The sanctuary is full of scattered pews and an organ crumbles into the floor in the corner.

Do you like it?

WASP: *(despite themself)* I mean . . . yeah. I do. Lots of potential. Cool stained glass.

ISAAC: Exactly. It's full of potential. There's a field out back that used to be the church garden. It's perfect for growing stuff. Full sunlight. Great drainage. I'm thinking corn, zucchini, and tomatoes. Maybe a greenhouse. This place'll take some work, but I think it'll make a nice little house once the renos are complete.

WASP: Last I checked you didn't even eat vegetables.

ISAAC: I don't, really. But you inspired me. The minute I saw this spot I thought: Wasp would love this.

WASP: *(uncomfortable)* So what's the surprise?

ISAAC: This is it. It's for you.

He hands them the deed.

WASP: You can't be serious.

ISAAC: Look, I know we've had our differences but—I don't want to lose you. You're still my best friend. After everything.

Beat.

I know this was a dream of yours. A little place of your own.

WASP: Really?

ISAAC: Just say yes. It's easy.

WASP slowly flips through the contract.

WASP: It says you bought this off the cult. For a dollar.

ISAAC: You're right. Not free: you owe me a dollar.

He moves closer to them. WASP feels the twist of disappointment in the pit of their stomach—here's the trap. An old dream brought to life.

WASP: Oh God.

ISAAC: It's not that bad, Wasp. Really. Everyone's nice, and there are snacks after church, and people genuinely care about what's going on in your life.

WASP: Yeah, but you're a man.

ISAAC: So? Caroline isn't a man and she's thriving.

Beat.

Look around, the world is going to shit. Forest fires, floods, inflation, plague. But our community doesn't have to be like that. We can buckle down and make something together. You could . . . start again. We'll pull some strings. You can put the past behind you. Confess. And move forward.

Beat.

You're stuck, Wasp. Everyone can see it. This is a way out.

WASP: Isaac, I'm gay!

ISAAC: Then why are you with J—?

They don't answer.

Fuck that, Wasp. Find a real man. I know this is what you want.

WASP: I don't want to be a housewife.

ISAAC: That's not what you were saying when we were together.

He comes up behind them. Touches their hair. He can't see their face, but we can.

I know you. You're just a little girl who wants to get fucked. Say it. Say it.

WASP: I—

ISAAC: Say it.

WASP: I'm just a little girl who wants to get fucked.

WASP tries to grab the keys from his belt. They miss. ISAAC is monologuing, impassioned.

ISAAC: Think about it . . . If I made love to you— If I made love to you so hard. If I was so deep within you that you just had to have a baby. And you came—this toe-breaking kind of orgasm: you'd cum and all your toes would go off like firecrackers.

And you wouldn't be able to walk 'cause all your toes would be broken but it would be okay because I'd pick you up—I really would—I'd pick you up and I'd take you anywhere in my arms. Anywhere you wanted, I really would.

People would say, sir, why are you carrying this woman, and I would say well, it's my destiny. It's my destiny. Don't you people know what DESTINY MEANS, and they wouldn't know that I'd saved you, but I would know. We would know and our baby would know and that would be enough.

WASP: Isaac . . .

He moves closer to them. He talks with his eyes closed.

ISAAC: It's not the same without you. It really isn't. I tried—I tried alone for a while and then I tried with Caroline, but you did this thing, Wasp, you messed me up inside.

Sometimes I get so in my head that I'll see a woman in the street and I'll stand beside her and slip my hand into hers because I think, *I think for a second that it's you.*

If it was you, I could hold your hand and we could be in love again for a split second and it would feel so good. It feels so good. Doesn't it?

WASP: Yes. It feels so good.

ISAAC starts to unzip his pants. WASP pulls the keys out of his pocket—he thinks that they're accepting his gift.

ISAAC: Good girl.

ISAAC starts to undress them. They're frozen, caught in a memory and the urgency of their plan with JANEY. Their eyes run around the room and suddenly land on the bottle of Coke. The weight of their rage returns to them.

WASP: Where did you get that?

ISAAC looks up from kissing their neck.

ISAAC: Oh, uh—

WASP: I haven't been able to find Coke anywhere. They pulled it out of all of the stores. Rachel said there was . . . a supply-chain problem.

ISAAC: Yeah. There was.

WASP: What, you bought them all?

ISAAC: It's the church. They're cracking down on sin.

WASP: And what sin would that be?

ISAAC: You of all people should know.

WASP: *(realizing)* Right. Just like Janey's birth control.

ISAAC: Who's birth control?

WASP: You told them. You told them about our abortion.

(to themself) Oh my God. She was right.

ISAAC: It's a bottle of pop, Wasp. It doesn't mean anything.

WASP: Great. Then you won't mind if I take this for myself.

> WASP *picks up the bottle of Coke. They walk towards the door.*

ISAAC: Wait, you're just gonna leave?

> WASP *keeps walking.* ISAAC *realizes what's happening. He tackles them.*

WASP: Get the fuck off of me!

ISAAC: Give me my keys!

> WASP *gets on top. They pull out their keys, which have a cool self-defence keychain and a canister of pepper spray attached. In hot pink, duh. They hit* ISAAC *with the keychain and he rolls away. They have the Coke under their arm.* ISAAC *has his keys now.*

What the fuck was that!

WASP: What the fuck is this? Conversion camp?

ISAAC: It's a gift!

WASP: With a million strings.

ISAAC: I love you, Wasp.

WASP: *(enraged)* Oh my God.

ISAAC: It's not what you think. Trust me. Come to my Divine Ceremony tonight. Hell, you can even bring J—. You'll see.

He pulls out his phone. They uncap the pepper spray.

WASP: Give me the keys.

ISAAC: Come on. This is ridiculous.

WASP: *(quietly)* No. You wanna know what's ridiculous? After? When you didn't call? I was worried that you were mad. I was afraid you didn't like me anymore. That's fucking ridiculous.

ISAAC: Wasp—

WASP: Give. Me. The. Keys.

ISAAC: *(a long beat)* I can't. I'm supposed to be picking up Rachel in ten.

WASP: So walk.

ISAAC: Sure, I'll just call ahead and tell them I'm being robbed.

WASP: Fuck.

Beat.

Get in the car.

WASP walks ISAAC out of the church, holding the pepper spray like a gun. They get into the car.

We're going to Phil's. You're gonna walk in, you're gonna go to the ATM, and you're going to get me four hundred dollars in cash. For J—'s bike.

ISAAC: Four hundred? That thing cost him forty bucks—

WASP: Then make it five. And if you don't do this, I will pepper spray the shit out of you and tell Caroline about all the times you cheated on her, including now when you tried to fuck me three hours before your wedding. Do you understand?

ISAAC: . . .

WASP: Say "I understand."

ISAAC: I understand.

They turn on the radio and sit in silence as ISAAC *drives them down to Phil's.* RACHEL *is still working.* ISAAC *goes to the* ATM *while* WASP *waits by the counter. They make eye contact with* RACHEL*, who is putting on her best lobotomized Jesus-believer act.*

RACHEL: Hi there, welcome to Phil's, would you like a pamphlet? We have: "Avoiding Sin in your Everyday Life!" Or, how about: "Male Virility and the All-Meat Diet."

WASP: Not today, Rachel.

RACHEL: Not to worry—there's something for everyone here. How about this one? "10 Reasons Why all Sodomites Will Burn in Eternal Hellfire."

(under her breath) Please. I have a quota to fill.

WASP: Load me up.

RACHEL: God bless you, lowly sinner.

(under her breath) What are you doing here?

WASP: Settling some debts.

ISAAC *comes back from the* ATM. *He leans across the counter towards* RACHEL.

ISAAC: *(ignoring* WASP*, to* RACHEL*)* Hey, punk, what do you think—can you sneak me some rolling papers on the house?

RACHEL: Stealing is a sin, *punk.*

ISAAC: I know. That's why I'm asking.

RACHEL: One pack. But you have to distribute these pamphlets. And roll me a cigarette.

WASP: The money, Isaac.

ISAAC: Here.

He hands them the cash.

I really think we can work this out, Wasp.

Beat.

Don't give up on me.

Overcome with disgust and shame, WASP *exits the store. As they leave, they hear* ISAAC *speak to* RACHEL*.*

(to RACHEL*)* Are you ready to go?

RACHEL: No.

Walking down the highway, WASP *counts their money. They realize that* ISAAC *shortchanged them.*

WASP: Twenty, forty, sixty, eighty—fuck! FUCK! Stupid.

They take out their phone and call JANEY*. She picks up immediately.*

He's a maniac. I don't know what he was on, some kind of recruitment shit.

JANEY: Recruitment shit? Slow down.

WASP: He tried to give me a farm, and when that didn't work he tried to fuck me, and then he was like, "*Let's have a family*!" Then I tried to get money for your bike, but he ripped me off—FUCK. FUCK!

JANEY: Where are you?

WASP: I'm walking home. I'll be there in like twenty. I'm sorry—

JANEY: Hey, you tried your best. Stealing cars is hard—

WASP hears the sound of a call waiting on the other line.

WASP: Someone's calling me.

JANEY: You think it's him?

WASP: It better not be. One sec.

They switch calls. On the other line is a slightly crackly and ominously cheerful voice.

PROPHET: Good afternoon, is this Wasp Noël?

We hear the sound of WASP breathing. They're frozen in fear.

Hi there, I'm calling to congratulate you on your decision to walk the righteous path and devote yourself to God and our Lord and Saviour Jesus Christ. As a blessing on your new life, you've been selected as a candidate for Divine Birthday. Congratulations.

WASP: I—I didn't apply.

PROPHET: We don't apply to Jesus, my dear. He chooses us. Your ceremony will take place tonight at the Altar at exactly midnight. Please dress appropriately. A nightgown or other white dress should suffice. It's recommended that you fast beforehand, though it isn't required. Do you have any questions?

WASP: . . . What happens if I don't show up?

PROPHET: No problem. We'll find you.
Midnight. Don't be late.

The line goes dead.

End of Act I.

[ACT 2, SCENE 5]

CAROLINE is escorted into a cold, empty room. On the wall is a massive TV. It flickers to life. On screen a video of her father, the PROPHET, in a smart suit. '90s infomercial style. Maybe in this moment the audience is the cult—and CAROLINE sits among them.

PROPHET: You were alone. You felt like other people just didn't get it.

You were depressed. Searching for meaning in your life. And then: you found us. Congratulations on dedicating your life to cultivating harmony and community for the greater good. Give yourself a round of applause.

CAROLINE claps fervently.

You've arrived at the moment. Today is your Divine Birthday. Now I know, you might be scared. You may even be unsure. But today is the day that you join us as a full member. You are no longer a child who relies on God's grace and the community's generosity to survive. Now you are a Holy Mother—a cornerstone of the community. Through your divine submission the Seraphim will reap new life.

Today you repay God by gifting Him your body.

If at any time you need anything, don't hesitate to call out—we, your chosen family, will be watching from the viewing room, and attendants will be on hand to best assist you in a comfortable Birthday process.

Now. It's time. You are the field in which God sows the future. Be blessed, and be brave.

Tinny music plays and the screen fades to black. We hear the PROPHET*'s disembodied voice.*

Caroline Abigail Stephens, are you prepared?

CAROLINE: I am.

PROPHET: Then enter, and be blessed.

She enters the Altar.

The sound of CAROLINE*'s feet on cold stone, echoing in a large, cavernous space. Building, ritualistic music à la "Choir" by Perfume Genius. Gothic, Christian, and sinister. In the centre of the room is a bathtub full of water—*CAROLINE *removes the ritual dress and gets into the tub. She stands, washing her body—preparing. She pours water over her head. A sense of immense calm and solemnity is with her. This is her moment.*

In a parallel to CAROLINE*'s ritual, we see* RACHEL*—hair coming loose, on the highway in the dark—*ISAAC*'s headlights shining on her. She has her back to him. The sound of a car door slamming.*

ISAAC: RACHEL! Come on, punk, don't do this. Think of Caroline.

RACHEL: Tell her I'm on my way.

ISAAC: It's an hour-long walk, you're going to miss the ceremony.

RACHEL: My new schedule allows me one hour of fresh air a day. I'm taking it.

ISAAC: You can breathe air later.

RACHEL: I don't need a fucking chaperone!

ISAAC: I'm not your chaperone—I'm your friend.

RACHEL: Fucking my sister doesn't make us friends.

ISAAC: Just get back in the car and we can pretend this never happened, okay?

RACHEL: *(sarcastic)* Be blessed, Isaac, tell Caroline I say hi.

RACHEL turns and runs into the forest.

ISAAC: RACHEL— RACHEL! MotherFUCKER.

ISAAC's running late, but losing RACHEL is unforgivable. He decides to chase after her.

At the Altar, the moment of the Divine Birthday is happening. CAROLINE is half-naked, steaming, lying on the marble slab, wrapped in the dress like a bride.

CAROLINE: Father, I give my body unto you
Take me in your winged embrace
Fill me with your seed
For I am the field of the future
I am the field of the future
Plant the seeds of the future
And let Him reap the fruit.

CAROLINE sits up. The music crescendos. The sound of many people humming together. CAROLINE hums deep in her throat. A grand moment as a door opens—ISAAC is supposed to enter. He's not there.

Isaac?

In the forest, ISAAC *catches up to* RACHEL.

ISAAC: Come here—

RACHEL: Get away from me!

We hear the familiar buzz of a yellowjacket: ISAAC *coughs. He coughs again. He starts to claw at his throat. A single wasp falls out of his mouth, covered in blood.*

ISAAC: What is that— WHAT'S HAPPENING TO ME?

RACHEL: You FUCKING IDIOT—

ISAAC *screams, horrified. More yellowjackets fly out of his mouth, straight at* RACHEL. *The ritual of the Divine Birthday begins in the woods. The sound of the swarm overtakes them. They are lost in the noise.*

At the Altar, CAROLINE *is left in bone-chilling silence.*

CAROLINE: ISAAC!?

The PROPHET*'s voice comes over the loudspeaker.*

PROPHET: Caroline Stephens?

CAROLINE: Father? Father, what's going on?

PROPHET: Please report to assessment room 201.

CAROLINE: No— He hasn't come yet. I'm still waiting.

PROPHET: Please report to assessment room 201.

CAROLINE: He's coming. He's just late!

PROPHET: You have been deemed unfit. Please report to assessment room 201.

CAROLINE: Unfit? No—no—I'm ready. *I'm ready—*

PROPHET: Your Divine Birthday has been terminated. Please exit the Altar.

A door opens. Congregants wearing surgical masks approach her, ready to escort her out.

CAROLINE: No. No! He's coming! No!

She kicks at them. They come forward and pick her up. They exit the room with CAROLINE *between their arms.*

[ACT 2, SCENE 6]

JANEY and WASP are looking at themselves in the mirror. Their usual punk/queer aesthetic has been replaced by them trying to dress "straight." They're both horrified—and they're not doing a great job looking straight. WASP is still wearing combat boots. JANEY has long painted nails. In the background, the Coke looms.

JANEY: What do hitchhikers even wear? We look like we're going to a picnic.

WASP: We're trying to look inviting . . . not—

JANEY: Gay? Straight couples own cars, Wasp. They don't walk along the highway with their thumbs out—

WASP pulls at the long flowy dress that they're wearing. JANEY adjusts her collar.

WASP: I feel like I'm going to gnaw my own arm off.

JANEY: Great. Food for the picnic.

WASP: Have you seen my jeans? The black ones?

WASP starts digging through piles of clothes on the bed. There's a franticness to them. The cash from ISAAC flutters to the ground.

JANEY: Wasp . . . you're spiralling.

WASP: It's not spiralling—it's called the flight or fight response and it's a perfectly natural part of the nervous system, thank you very much—

JANEY touches them gently on the arm.

JANEY: You already packed your black jeans. Let's make a list, okay? Three shirts, seven pairs of underwear, eight pairs of socks. Two bottoms. One special occasion thing.

WASP: No. We don't have any room.

JANEY: Why don't you bring that harness you made?

WASP: I don't think I'm going to need a leather harness—

JANEY: Who knows where we're going? Maybe it'll be the dress code in the big city. And we'll get there and you'll be like, oh shit, my harness! And they'll be like, sorry, you can't come in, no straight people allowed.

WASP: Who's managing this, gay cops?

JANEY: It makes you feel special. Pack it. Okay?

JANEY goes back to packing. WASP looks at the harness for a long time. Suddenly they're crying.

WASP: He fucking got me. There was this moment where I could see it. The house, the garden, the family. I . . . I felt her there, between us. I never feel her anymore.

JANEY: I know, baby. And he knew that.

WASP: *(looking at the bottle of Coke)* We should pack this too. Just in case.

JANEY: Sure. But we'll be long gone by midnight. And when the sun comes up on the next town, we can drink the Coke to celebrate.

WASP: *(laughing)* Ew.

Beat.

I don't want to go.

JANEY: Me neither. But I'm glad I'm going with you.

WASP: I love you.

JANEY: I love you too. And it's an honour.

(changing tone) But, babe, you really don't need that many shirts.

WASP: *(laughing)* Fuck!

JANEY: You sit, I pack.

Headlights glide across their wall, a car door slams. Pounding on their door: someone's outside. JANEY *and* WASP *go downstairs to look through the keyhole—they can hear* ISAAC *through the door. His voice sounds strange.*

Not this fuck again.

ISAAC: WASP—WASP—I know you're in there. LET ME IN. Let me in. Please.

WASP: Something's wrong. He should be at the Altar.

ISAAC *collapses in the doorway, wheezing and sniffling.*

JANEY: Is he crying?

ISAAC: I fucked up—please, I need your help. PLEASE—

WASP opens the door. ISAAC is sitting on their front step, clutching his chest. His neck and face are swollen with wasp stings.

(wheezing) I can't breathe. I can't breathe—

WASP: Janey, get the EpiPen—

JANEY hands WASP an EpiPen. They look at ISAAC for a moment and then stab him in the leg with it. He cries out.

ISAAC: FUCK!

WASP: I'll add that to your tab.

ISAAC inhales deeply as his windpipe opens. He gasps, relieved.

ISAAC: You saved me. Thank you—

He tries to grab their leg. They kick him back.

WASP: Don't fucking touch me. You have ten minutes to get off our porch.

They go to close the door. ISAAC starts laughing as the adrenaline hits his body.

ISAAC: You knew. You knew this was gonna happen. Didn't you, J—? That's why you opted out. I don't blame you.

JANEY: You don't know anything about me.

ISAAC: *(to WASP)* Did you know? Huh?

WASP: Know what, Isaac?

ISAAC: This! That they would do THIS TO ME.

He gestures at his swollen face, spits off their porch.

It was so fucked up.

She ran into the woods, and I was like, fuck, I can't leave her here, but by the time I found her it was nine. I thought it was a joke. A fantasy. But the look on her face. Like I was a monster. And then I felt them. Coming out of me.

He shudders.

JANEY: Wait—who did you follow into the woods?

ISAAC: *(to himself)* She's gonna kill me.

JANEY: Isaac. Look at me. Who did you follow into the woods?

ISAAC: *(crying)* She's gonna fucking kill me.

WASP: No. I saw him leaving with—with . . . Rachel.

JANEY: No—

ISAAC: *(quietly)* She's in the back.

JANEY opens ISAAC's car door. Inside we can see a figure sprawled in the back seat, clearly unconscious and extremely pregnant. It's RACHEL.

JANEY: Oh FUCK NO.

ISAAC: It was an accident—

JANEY: An accident? What, were you just running a few minutes late and you happened to IMPREGNATE HER?

ISAAC: She jumped out of the car. She was trying to escape.

JANEY: Escape you, maybe.

ISAAC: I didn't know. I didn't read the handbook.

JANEY: Spare me the innocence—you signed the covenant!

ISAAC: I have dyslexia! Okay?

WASP has been looking at RACHEL.

WASP: So why are you here?

ISAAC: I need your help.

WASP: Lots of people have EpiPens.

ISAAC: Not like that. She wants an abortion.

WASP looks at him with pure hatred.

WASP: Right. Of course.

ISAAC: I'll do it—just tell me what to do. You can . . . supervise.

WASP: No.

ISAAC: So you think I should take her to the Altar then? See what they do to us? (*gestures at JANEY*) J— knows. They'll lock her up.

WASP: What about you?

JANEY: (*tightly*) He'll be fine.

WASP pulls JANEY aside.

WASP: I don't like this. What if they sent him to take me?

JANEY: No one's done two rounds in one night before. Look at him. He's only alive 'cause we saved him.

WASP: I don't even know if I can help her. She's so far along—

JANEY: He has a car, and he has Rachel. That's all that matters.

WASP: Stealing cars is hard!

JANEY: Yeah, but three against one is easier.

Beat.

We can't just leave her with him.

WASP: I know. I know.

They both look at RACHEL.

ISAAC: Do you think she's okay?

JANEY: *(snapping)* She's unconscious and pregnant in the back of your car, Isaac. So I'm gonna go out on a limb and say she's not doing great.

ISAAC *grabs* RACHEL *and shakes her, in a panicky way.*

ISAAC: Rachel. Rachel? Hello?

JANEY: Easy.

ISAAC: She's gonna wake up, right?

WASP: She needs a minute.

ISAAC: She's had a minute.

WASP: So she needs another one.

ISAAC: We can't stay here—someone's going to see. We have to move her.

JANEY: Do you have a blanket or something we can cover her with?

ISAAC: Uh . . . There are garbage bags in the trunk.

JANEY: Wow. King of hospitality over here.

WASP: *(taking a deep breath)* He's right. We need to get out of here before someone sees.

ISAAC: You're gonna come with us?

JANEY: No, Isaac. We're gonna leave you alone with an unconscious girl and a two litre bottle of Coke.

> *Beat.*

Get in the car.

> *WASP goes back towards the house. JANEY puts ISAAC in the back with RACHEL.*

ISAAC: I can drive.

JANEY: Not on epinephrine you can't. Hand 'em over.

> *A long beat. He hands her the keys.*

ISAAC: I have a spot, just off the highway. We'll go there.

JANEY: Oh I know all about your spot, Isaac.

JANEY closes the door on him. WASP comes downstairs with a box of supplies and both of their backpacks. They're catching their ride. WASP puts their bags in the trunk and kisses JANEY.

[ACT 2, SCENE 7]

JANEY and WASP are playing cards. ISAAC is pacing behind them anxiously. RACHEL is still unconscious, lying on some blankets near the pulpit—very Altar-like. The bell tolls 11 p.m. Everyone is antsy. A lot of tension.

ISAAC: If she doesn't wake up soon, we're gonna have to just do it.

WASP: So that's your plan, do a Coca-Cola abortion on her while she's unconscious?

ISAAC: . . . No? No. Of course not.

JANEY: Do you have any nines?

WASP: Go fish.

JANEY: *(to ISAAC)* You've got to stop pacing—you're giving me anxiety.

WASP: Do you have any fours?

JANEY: Go fish.

ISAAC: Do you hear that?

WASP: Hear what?

ISAAC: That buzzing.

JANEY: No. I don't hear anything.

ISAAC gets up, starts listening to RACHEL's stomach.

ISAAC: I think it's coming from inside her.

JANEY: Are you high?

ISAAC: Listen! LISTEN—do you hear that? It's like . . . a humming. I swear. Shhh!

We all listen. We don't hear anything.

WASP: I don't hear anything. Sit down.

ISAAC: As long as those things are inside her, we're not safe.

JANEY: I mean technically "those things" came from you, so wouldn't that mean you're / not safe?

ISAAC: Oh yeah. Go ahead. Blame me. I'm just as fucked up as she is.

A long beat. JANEY and WASP stare at ISAAC and the ridiculousness of this statement. Finally he gets embarrassed.

(clears throat) Do you have any fives?

JANEY: Go fucking fish.

ISAAC: Okay, but look at her—she's huge. We're going to have a baby on our hands in a few hours. Do you want to murder a baby?

WASP: I want to murder *you.*

ISAAC: When you did it. Last time. What did you do? Tell me.

WASP: I mean, you would know if you were there. But as I remember you couldn't fit it into your busy schedule of being a fuckass . . .

ISAAC: We've been over this—they booked me overtime at work.

WASP: Right, and then after work, they booked you overtime at the bar, yeah?

ISAAC: Oh fuck you.

WASP: No thanks.

JANEY: Do you have any eights?

ISAAC throws down three eights with venom.

ISAAC: Fold.

JANEY: You can't fold, it's Go Fish.

ISAAC walks over to their supplies. He looks it over. Coke, a thing of Mentos, a lot of medical gauze, Tylenol 3s, a joint. A pair of black gloves (clearly for fisting). He suddenly seems more dangerous.

ISAAC: So what, you just put the Coke up there and then wait for it to come out? Like a fetus Slip 'N Slide?

JANEY: Oh, spare us.

ISAAC: Tell me.

Beat.

TELL ME!

WASP: It takes time. She's going to miscarry for hours and it's going to hurt like a bitch. And this time you'll be here to watch the whole thing.

ISAAC: Hours? We don't have hours. I'm waking her up. Now. Wake up, Rachel. Wake up!

He starts kicking shit, making noise, banging on pipes. When this doesn't work he grabs her leg, starts putting her into a stirrup position.

WASP: Don't fucking touch her, Isaac.

ISAAC: You don't like it? Then come help me.

They watch him, arms crossed.

No? Fine. I'll improvise—what do you think, should ten Mentos do it?

He grabs the Coke.

Here goes nothing.

WASP: OKAY. Okay.

Beat.

Don't open that, we only have one shot.

JANEY gets down on her knees next to RACHEL. She smooths her hair back from her face.

JANEY: Rachel. Wake up. Please. Please wake up.

RACHEL doesn't wake. JANEY looks at WASP.

I don't know what else to do.

WASP: Okay. On the count of three, Janey, you open the Coke. Isaac: three Mentos. I'll move her underwear and then . . . we insert. One, two, three.

JANEY opens the Coke, ISAAC drops the Mentos in, but before WASP can touch her, RACHEL wakes up. The Coke sprays into ISAAC's face. He reels back.

ISAAC: Jesus Christ!!!!

RACHEL: WHAT THE FUCK IS GOING ON—

ISAAC: *(spitting out Coke)* Rachel, I need you to lie back down, we're running out of carbonation—

RACHEL: Carbonation? Carbonation for what?

ISAAC: I got you pregnant— *The Angels* got you pregnant, but don't worry, we're gonna fix this. Just breathe.

He grabs the Coke out of JANEY's hands and lunges forward. RACHEL scoots away.

RACHEL: What no—no—stop!

Everyone stops. The sound of Coke fizzing.

ISAAC: You asked for help! We're helping!

RACHEL: Since when does THIS mean help?

RACHEL gestures at the Coke all over her.

God, this shit is everywhere.

WASP: Isaac. You said she wanted this—

ISAAC: She does. She's just confused.

RACHEL takes off her Coke-stained sweater—we see the stings all over her arms. She touches them.

RACHEL: *(choked)* I asked, once. What it was like? My dad said that it would be like heaven. I didn't sleep for weeks 'cause I thought I was gonna die. But here we are. Made it.

She takes a deep breath and then runs her hands over her stomach.

Oh. Hi.
You're new.
(gasps) She kicked me.

Beat.

What do we think, is this heaven?

JANEY: *(looking at ISAAC)* Not as long as he's here.

RACHEL: I feel like I got hit by a truck. How long was I out?

JANEY: Too long.

JANEY hugs her.

ISAAC: Rachel: listen to me. I know you're upset. Lie back down and let us help you.

WASP: The bottle's flat. It's not going to work.

ISAAC: I have another.

JANEY: Now he tells us—

ISAAC: *(to RACHEL)* We can fix this. We're going to give you an abortion.

RACHEL: An abortion? Who said I wanted an abortion—

ISAAC: Everyone wants an abortion! Isn't that what feminism is?

WASP: *(to ISAAC)* What the fuck kind of game are you playing at?

RACHEL: *(to JANEY)* I told you. I tried everything—everything imaginable—and they still wouldn't let me go. But this is it. This is what'll get me out, and it was an accident.

JANEY: Breeding as the ultimate sin. God works in mysterious ways.

ISAAC: It's my choice too.

RACHEL: Yeah. It was. Your choice.
You joined the cult. You took the pills. And now you see the consequences.
All I wanted was my one hour of fresh fucking air.

RACHEL grabs WASP and JANEY's hands. All three of them start to back towards the door.

ISAAC: You can't just leave! That's my fetus in there and there is no way in HELL—

ISAAC strides across the room to RACHEL. WASP and JANEY go to intercept, but a frenzied knock on the door catches them all off guard.

CAROLINE: Isaac, open up! I know you're in there.

The sound of bolt cutters on the lock outside.

JANEY: Did she bring bolt cutters?

RACHEL: Fucking Caroline.

ISAAC: Everyone hide.

They don't move.

HIDE. And don't you dare leave. We're not done here.

They hide. The door opens.

CAROLINE stands in the doorway. She advances towards ISAAC. Her energy is electric. She's still wearing the Altar dress.

CAROLINE: Who are you talking to?

ISAAC: No one.

CAROLINE: Lying is a sin, Isaac. Where is she? Where's your fucking concubine?

ISAAC: Caroline. I can explain.

CAROLINE: I bought you ten cartons of eggs. I talked to Father. I read you the entire Bible. I set six reminders in your phone. So please, tell me, where did I go wrong? Should I have picked you up and driven you there myself? Or was she too much of a temptation? Hello? Wasp? Are you here? Sorry to interrupt—

WASP: *(whispering)* What the fuck . . .

JANEY: *(whispering)* I told you it was a set-up!

ISAAC: I know you're upset. I can explain.

CAROLINE: You signed a covenant, Isaac. You took a sacred vow. And I was supposed to be first.

ISAAC: Caroline, listen to me. Listen to me. She said no. It didn't happen.

CAROLINE: It didn't happen?

Beat.

Oh.

Beat.

Really?

JANEY: That's why you got the call. He chose you.

WASP: She was just another way to lure me back here.

RACHEL: Do we have an escape plan?

JANEY shows her ISAAC's keys.

JANEY: You'd better fucking believe it.

WASP, JANEY, and RACHEL start creeping towards the exit.

ISAAC: Really. I-I got scared. So I just jerked off instead.

CAROLINE: You masturbated instead of coming to my Divine Birthday.

ISAAC: I mean. It's probably for the best. You can't really want those things . . . inside you. Right?

CAROLINE: Those things? You mean the Angels? Of course I want them inside me. You took their eggs this morning. What did you think those tablets were?

ISAAC: Prenatal . . . vitamins?

CAROLINE: So this whole time you've just been going along with what I said, and you didn't even think it was real?

ISAAC: Fuck. FUCK!

CAROLINE: Stop cursing!

CAROLINE snaps at ISAAC, then starts pivoting. She needs her plan to work. ISAAC laughs in fear, starts backing up.

Well. Now you understand. And if she said no, then we still have midnight. So—let's just do it here. Who needs the Altar, right?

She laughs hysterically.

God's everywhere. And then, we can go back. With our baby. And they'll know we're forgiven. And it'll be fine.

ISAAC: Caroline, I think I'm allergic to Angels—

CAROLINE: No problem. I came prepared.

She pulls out two EpiPens.

You know how to use this, right? Blue to the sky, orange to the thigh.

She starts to caress his hair, take off his shirt. He resists.

This is your fantasy, Isaac. Having sex in our church. Where do you want me? In the pulpit, on the steps, in the pews?

ISAAC: I'm not really in the mood right now.

CAROLINE: *(feral)* So get in the mood.

ISAAC: Caroline—

CAROLINE: Yes, yes. I'll suck you off. But this time instead of coming on my back or my stomach, or on my face or in my eyes, when the bell tolls twelve, just put it in. Don't let a single Angel escape. Perfect perfect.

ISAAC: Perfect perfect.

> *WASP, JANEY, and RACHEL are sneaking towards the front of the building, under the pews. There's no way to the exit without them being seen. CAROLINE pauses—she hears them.*

CAROLINE: Hello? Who's there?

> *They stay still. We hear them breathing.*

ISAAC: It's no one. It's just me.

CAROLINE: Shut UP!

> *CAROLINE starts walking through the pews, getting closer and closer to WASP. They can see her feet. Then she stops.*

RACHEL: *(to WASP and JANEY)* Time for a diversion.

> *RACHEL steps out.*

Hi, Caroline.

CAROLINE: Rachel? What are you doing here? I thought you were—

RACHEL: Under house arrest?

CAROLINE: Learning. You know it's for your own good.

RACHEL: Right. Tell yourself that if it helps you sleep at night.

CAROLINE: You wanted to be found out. Dad's office? Come on.

RACHEL: Yeah. I did. I just didn't think you'd tell them.

CAROLINE: My candidacy was at risk. No sinners—just look at you.

RACHEL: Yeah. Look at me.

> *RACHEL walks towards her—CAROLINE sees a single yellowjacket sting on her cheek. She sees her pregnant stomach. She understands that ISAAC took her. If the actor felt so inclined, she could scream. Then:*

CAROLINE: (*choked*) Father will be so disappointed.

RACHEL: Finally.

> *CAROLINE smacks RACHEL across the face. RACHEL staggers back.*

ISAAC: Caroline.

CAROLINE: I can't believe you did this. You ruined everything.

> *WASP and JANEY pop up from the pews—they grab RACHEL and the three of them run out the door.*

ISAAC, what the HELL IS GOING ON?

WASP: Janey, time check?

JANEY: 11:56, babe.

> *JANEY holds up the keys.*

Let's get the fuck out of here.

> *They all get in the car. ISAAC runs out after them. JANEY locks the car doors.*

ISAAC: Wasp—Wasp, it's not like it seems. I wasn't going to take you—I promise. Please. Don't leave me here. I know I'm fucked up, but I can change.

I can. I swear. This isn't what I want.

A long beat. WASP *looks him up and down. Finally, they see everything.*

WASP: So apologize.

ISAAC: What?

WASP: Apologize to me. For everything.

ISAAC: I—I love you.

WASP: That's not good enough.

JANEY *backs up the car and they pull out of the parking lot, leaving* ISAAC *standing in the dust. He watches them go. It's 11:59.* CAROLINE *steps out of the church behind* ISAAC. *He turns and tries to take her hand.*

ISAAC: *(choked up)* I'm sorry.

CAROLINE: Let's get this over with.

A light glows down on him as he enters the church. The sound of a yellowjacket trapped in a glass.

The End.

ACKNOWLEDGEMENTS

This show has been my shadow since I was twenty years old, when Nightswimming commissioned it as part of their 5x25 program, dedicated to kick-starting the careers of five creators born in 1995. The day that Brian called me to give me the news, I was sitting (dissociating) at my office job in Montreal. When he told me I'd been selected, I think my exact words were, "No fucking way." And of course Brian, being Brian, simply said, "Yes, yes way," and, "Where can we send the cheque?" Three days earlier I had tried to buy a grilled-cheese sandwich and my card was declined; now I was a playwright, with a paycheque from a company. This is how my artistic career began—with a breath of financial stability and through a life-changing collaboration with the most patient and generous company I could dream of. Thank you, Brian, Brittany, and Nightswimming for being there as I grew up and into myself as a writer and a person. You changed my life.

Thank you to Gabe Maharjan for holding my hand through the final draft and telling me that things made sense. To Cole Alvis, who suggested that the ending be more gay. To Brandon Crone, producer extraordinaire: I couldn't do this without you. To Heath V. Salazar and Robin Luckwaldt, who've lent their genius minds to this ride since 2018. To Amaka Umeh, Brefny Caribou, and Jillian Harris for being such generous collaborators. To Ren Bangert, for their audio skills and love of all things horror. To Trevor Barrette and Katherine Belyea: stage managers make the world go ROUND.

Thanks to everyone who read this play aloud in its infancy between 2016–2019: in Montreal, Toronto, attics, basements, bedrooms. Thanks to everyone who listened. I appreciate you all.

Additional thank yous to ted witzel, the Stratford Festival Lab, the Canada Council for the Arts, the Toronto Arts Council, lemonTree creations, safeword, Playwrights Canada Press, Buddies in Bad Times Theatre, James Knott, the Rose Festival, Stephen Jackman-Torkoff, Khadijah Roberts-Abdullah, Christine Quintana (for being a champion), Kira Buro (who did the amazing cover), Nel Meyrink (for your multi-faceted and life-changing wisdom), Maybe McInnis (for living with me through drafts one, two, and three and being there during the Grilled Cheese Incident), and Jess (for saying you liked the show). Thanks to Blake and Annie at Playwrights Canada Press for publishing my unproduced play, and for their patience and respect for my mental health. Thanks to my family: to my grandma for telling me not to get married, and to my parents and my sibling for their open-mindedness and constant support in all of my professional endeavours. Thanks to David Beare and Tracey Lloyd, who introduced me to the world of theatre.

Most of all thanks to Wasp, Janey, Rachel, Caroline, and Isaac, for whispering in my ear and teaching me all the complexities of love. I hope you find your way.

Rhiannon Collett (they/them) is a playwright, performer, and translator based in Vancouver on the territories of the Squamish, Musqueam, and Tsleil-Waututh nations. They are interested in interdisciplinary creation processes, sexual labour, gender performativity, and science fiction. Selected playwriting credits include *Miranda & Dave Begin Again* (Playwrights Guild of Canada RBC Emerging Playwright Award), *Wasp* (Nightswimming/safeword), *The Kissing Game* (Youtheatre/Young People's Theatre), *J'ai Jamais* (French translation by Pénélope Bourque, Youtheatre/Télé-Québec/Maison Théâtre) and *Girlfriend* (Young People's Theatre).